Forget-Me-Not

Ho Phi Le

This lovely book is dedicated to:

Mary Ruddell
Ted Menten
Nancy Sandberg

Additional copies of this book may be purchased at $14.95 from
HOBBY HOUSE PRESS, INC.
1 Corporate Drive
Grantsville, Maryland 21536
1-800-554-1447
(please add $4.75 per copy for postage)
or from your favorite bookstore or dealer.

© 1994 Ho Phi Le

Printed in the United States of America

ISBN: 0-87588-425-3

Gentle Thoughts...

Isn't it the truth that the space of time
tends to let us forget
the child within our hearts.
Let's not run away from our childhood dreams,
instead we need to nurture
and embrace the memories of a happy
and innocent time in our lives.
Through the flight of our imagination,
let the day take us to wherever we want to be.

I hope FORGET-ME-NOT
will open another window in your soul,
and the images that I have captured here
will touch your heart in a gentle way.

Ho Phi Le

Once upon a dream...
where your childhood memories
are only a gentle touch away.

Stay as sweet as you are
Through your innocent years,
Be as gentle as you can be
With those you love so dearly,
Share your heavenly smiles
With the world you live in,
Never give up your dreams
For dreams will never die.

Ho Phi Le

"*You and I*
        together, Love,
never mind
        the weather, Love."

H. Winn

If you have a smile to show,
Show it now,
Make hearts happy, roses grow,
Let the friends around you know
The love you have before they go;
Show it now.

G. Klingle

Do I love thee?
Ask the flower
If she loves the vernal shower.
Or the kisses of the sun,
Or the dew when the day is done.
As she answers,
yes or no...
Darling
take my answer so.

T.G. Saxe

Smile!
The world is blue enough
Without your feeling blue.
Smile!
There's not half joy enough
Unless you're happy too.
Smile!
The sun is always shining
And there's work to do.
Smile!
This world may not be Heaven,
But then it's Home to you.

E.O.G.

Friendship, a star
Which moves not mid
The morning heavens alone,
A smile among dark frowns,
A gentle tone
Among rude voices,
A beloved light,
A solitude, a refuge, a delight.

Shelley

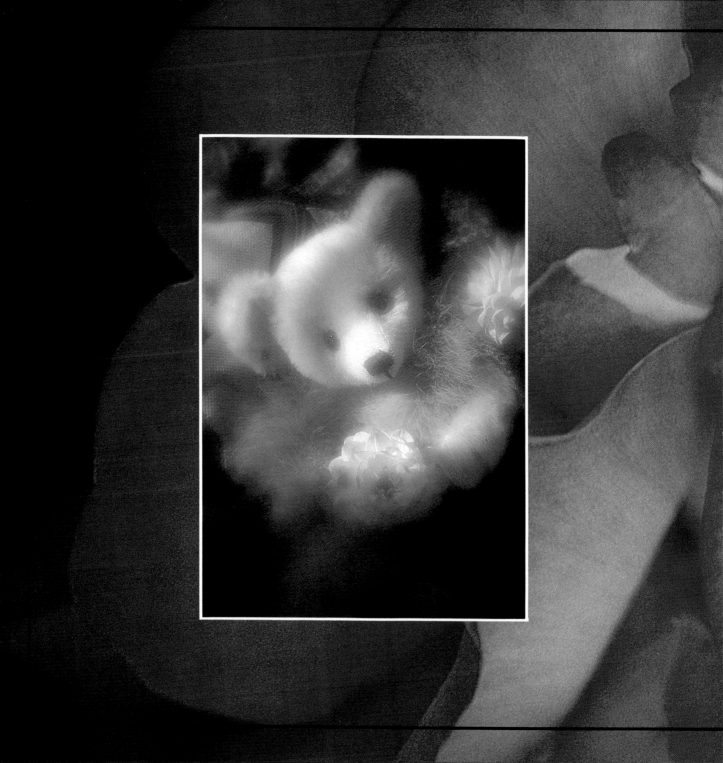

*Look for a lovely thing
and you will find it,
It is not far...
It will never be far.*

Sara Teasdale

*Life has taught us
that love does not consist of gazing at each other,
but in looking outward together in the same direction.*

Antoine de St.-Exupery

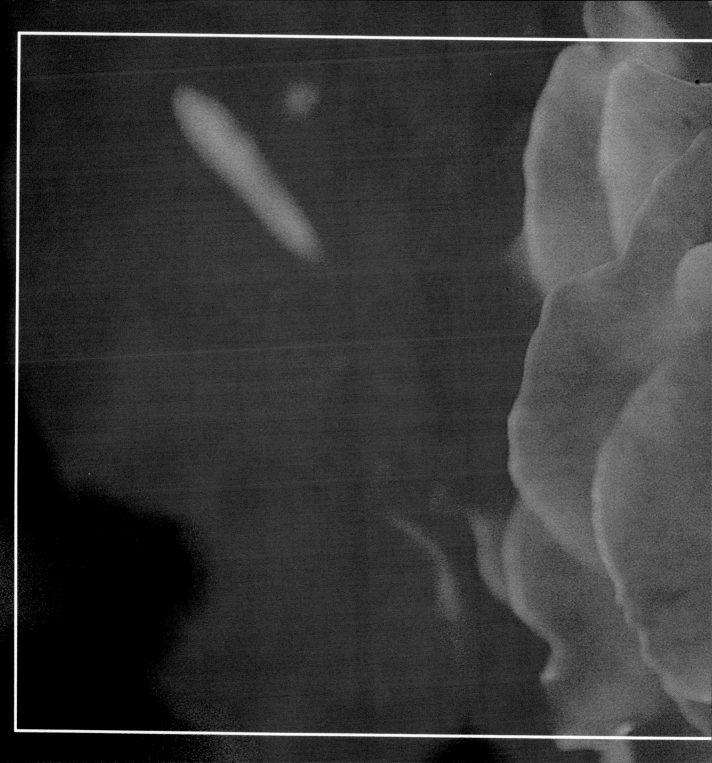

*Oh my love's
like a red,
red rose
That's newly
sprung in June;*

*Oh my love's
like a melodie
That's sweetly
played in tune.*

Burns

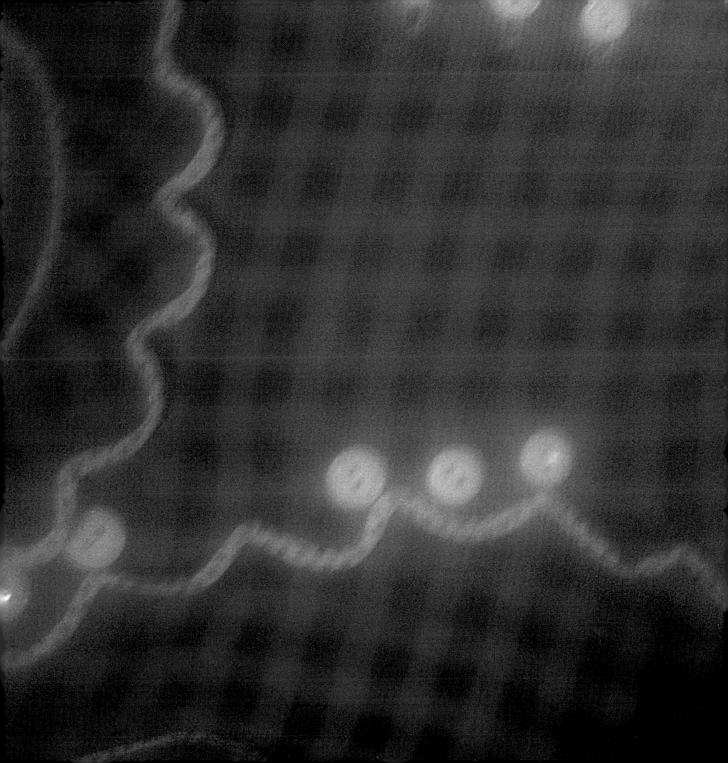

Red is the color of my heart,
That opens the window of my soul,
So long as...
Love me true.

Ho Phi Le

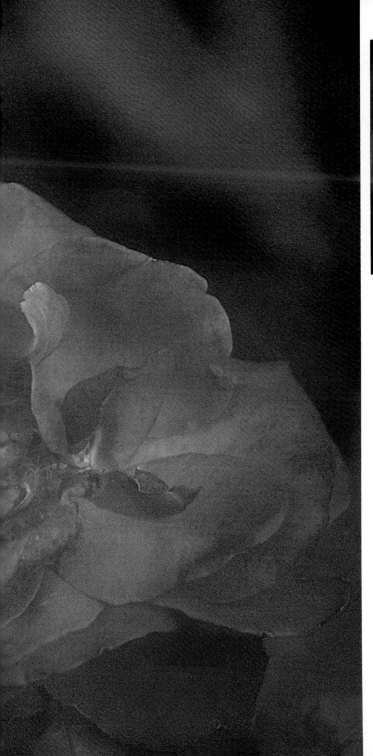

When time,
who steals
our years away,
Shall steal
our pleasures too,
The memory
of the past
will stay
And
half our joys renew.

Moore

*If one truly loves Nature,
he will find beauty everywhere.*

Vincent van Gogh

There is only one happiness in life,
to love and be loved.

George Sand

The sweetest music ever heard,
The sweetest perfume ever stirred,
Cannot compare with this dear word:
The simple, sweet "God bless you."

Of all who offer you friendship
Let me ever be the first,
The truest, the nearest, and dearest.

Longfellow

Could you have seen the violets
That blossomed in her eyes;
Could you have kissed that golden hair
And drank those holy sighs,
Oh you'd have been her tiring maid
As joyfully as I.

Unknown

They might not need me,
yet they might,
I'll let my heart be just in sight.
A smile so small as mine might be
Precisely their necessity.

Emily Dickinson

Come live with me
and be my love,
And we will all
the pleasures prove,
That valleys, groves,
hills and fields,
Woods and steepy
mountain yields.

Christopher Marlowe

Shall I compare thee
to a summer's day?
Thou art more lovely
and more temperate:
Rough winds do shake
the darling buds of May,
And summer's lease hatch
all too short a date...

William Shakespeare

What a heavenly feeling it is,
to follow one's heart.

Johann Wolfgang von Goethe

Danny's Fairy

Danny's fairy
Laughing with all her might
Oh, Danny's fairy
Can't stop making
Those happy melodies.

Ho Phi Le

*If you have
a song
to sing
Sing it now.
Let the tones
of gladness
ring,
Clear as song
of bird
in spring.
Let every day
some music
bring;
Sing it now.*

If you have
kind words
to say,
Say them now.
Tomorrow
may not come
your way,
Do a kindness
while you may;
Loved ones
will not always
stay,
Say them now.

G. Klingle

Heart to Heart

Tender and true, Dear...I never forget you!
And now when above us
the skies are grown blue,

With warmest affection
the heart where I set you,
Like flowers to the sunshine
is turning to you.

Unknown

The Old Window-Seat

In the old Nursery window-seat
They played one happy day,
They heard the ploughboy in the
wheat,
The sailors in the bay.

"And I will be a sailor too,
And sail the stormy sea,"
"And what am I at home to do
When you are gone?" said she.

"I will you all my toys," he said,
And took her dimpled hand,
"And you will play along the bay
And see the sailors land.
And once you'll see a vessel tall,
The captain I shall be!"
"But will you love me best of all
As you do now?" said she.

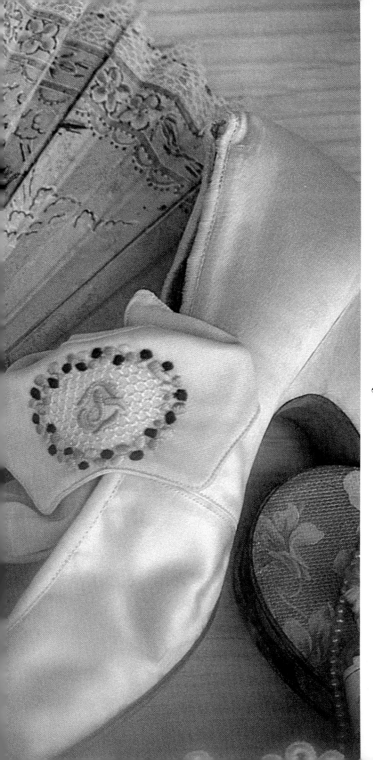

. . .

In the old Nursery window-seat
After long years they stand,
They see the bay, the ships, the
wheat,
The home of Nursery-land,

He bends him o'er her golden head,
She lifts her eyes of blue,
"The Nursery-land is best," he said,
"Because it gave me you!"

Frederic E. Weatherly

Side by side,
By the waves of the ocean blue,
You taught me how to find a perfect shell,

Somehow...
I did find more than just beautiful empty shells,
I've found the love that you've given me...
So unconditionally.

Ho Phi Le

Let me take you by the sea,
my little dear son,
for a day of sunshine and happiness.

Together,
you and I
will make this day
a lasting memory;
just you and me
for eternity...

Ho Phi Le

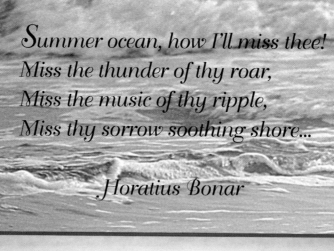

Summer ocean, how I'll miss thee!
Miss the thunder of thy roar,
Miss the music of thy ripple,
Miss thy sorrow soothing shore...

Horatius Bonar

The song-bird seeks its nest,
The sun sinks in the west,
And kindly thoughts are speeding to you.
May Joy with you abide,
May Hope be aye your guide,
And Love protect you,
All life's journey through.

Burnside

The tide recedes but leaves behind
bright seashells on the sand,
The sun goes down,
but gentle warmth still lingers on the land,
The music stops,
and yet it echoes on in sweet refrains...
For every joy that passes,
something beautiful remains.

H. Marshall

A Heartfelt Thank You...

Mary and Gary Ruddell for giving me a chance to work on the design of this lovely book.
Mary Beth Ruddell for being my editor.
Carolyn Cook for her support and friendship.
Ted Menten for believing in me from the start.
Nancy Sandberg for her unconditional love.
Jim Fernando for his friendship and love for dolls.
Barrie and Danny Shapiro for being such a sweet couple.
Lisa Lichtenfels for her incredible artistry in soft sculpture.
Susan Krey for her talents and for loving Asian children.
Anna Taccino for her beautiful lavender.
To my sister Diep and her daughter Raeann, Hazel Coons, Connie and Evan, Carolyn Stone,
Trever Dowse, Michelle Lemieux, Kristina Baker, Cindy Martin, Cathie Levy, Debbie and Mike
Schramer, Jeanette Warner, Julie and Susan Scott, Barbara Lauver, Dottie Ayers, Rosalie and Julia
Whyel, and most of all to my best friend Paul Hardin.